MACMILLAN READERS

INTERMEDIATE LEVEL

JOE SIMPSON

Touching the Void

Retold by Anne Collins

INTERMEDIATE LEVEL

Founding Editor: John Milne

The Macmillan Readers provide a choice of enjoyable reading materials for learners of English. The series is published at six levels – Starter, Beginner, Elementary, Pre-intermediate, Intermediate and Upper.

Level Control
Information, structure and vocabulary are controlled to suit the students' ability at each level.

The number of words at each level:

Starter	about 300 basic words
Beginner	about 600 basic words
Elementary	about 1100 basic words
Pre-intermediate	about 1400 basic words
Intermediate	about 1600 basic words
Upper	about 2200 basic words

Vocabulary
Some difficult words and phrases in this book are important for understanding the story. Some of these words are explained in the story, some are shown in the pictures, and others are marked with a number like this: ...³. Words with a number are explained in the Glossary at the end of the book.

Answer Keys
Answer Keys for the *Points for Understanding* and *Exercises* sections can be found at www.macmillanenglish.com/readers

Contents

A Note About the Author

Joe Simpson never intended to be a writer. He always wanted to be a mountaineer and climb mountains all over the world. But in 1985 at the age of 25, he had a terrible accident on Siula Grande, a mountain in the Peruvian Andes. The story of this accident is told in *Touching the Void*, which has become an international bestseller. Since the accident happened, Joe has become a successful author of novels as well as  non-fiction books. His books have won several major literary awards and prizes.

Joe did a degree in English Literature and Philosophy and has always liked writing. He is very good at making his stories seem real, even for people who have never climbed mountains. He describes his experiences on the mountains so well that we imagine we are there too. Joe has also become a well-known speaker, talking about *Touching the Void* first to the general public and people in the climbing world. Later he became a corporate speaker, giving talks to businesspeople.

Many people think that it was the accident in Peru which changed Joe's life, but Joe disagrees. He says that it was the success of *Touching the Void* which did this. He decided to write the book because there were many rumours[1] about what happened on Siula Grande to him and his climbing partner, Simon Yates. Not all these rumours were true and Joe wanted people to know the truth.

Joe lives in Sheffield in the UK. He enjoys many activities that are not as dangerous as climbing mountains, such as fishing in Ireland. He has been very pleased and surprised by his success as an author, but he also knows that life can change quickly. He has lost several friends who have been killed in climbing accidents. A climber can fall off a mountain when he is about to reach the summit, and it is the same with life. As Joe says, 'Life tends to go up and down. When you are at the top you always know that you could go screaming back down.'

A Note About the Story

Touching the Void is an extraordinary story of a person's courage[2] and ability to survive[3] in a very difficult situation. Many people have enjoyed the book because it is not just about mountain climbing, it is also a very good story. It could take place in any other type of lonely and difficult environment – like a desert or jungle. It deals with subjects that are interesting to all of us, like friendship, trust, loneliness and how human beings cope[4] when they think they are going to die.

Joe thought for a long time about a good title for his book. At first he wrote down ordinary words like 'loneliness', 'fear' and 'pain'. Finally he chose 'void' because it suggests terrible loss and emptiness, as well as a sense of being completely alone.

Touching the Void was made into a very successful film which won a BAFTA (British Academy Film and Television Arts) in 2004. During the making of the film, Joe had to go back to Peru for the first time in 17 years. When he revisited the place where he had nearly died, he suffered strong emotional stress. But when he saw the film for the first time, Joe was very pleased. He later felt as surprised about the huge success of the film as he was about the book.

You can find further information about Joe and *Touching the Void* on Joe's website, which is www.noordinaryjoe.com

Measurements: 1 foot = 30cm, 1 mile = 1.609 kilometres.

The West Face of Siula Grande

Climbing equipment

helmet

axe

rucksack

rope   crampon

Camping equipment

tent

pan

sleeping
bag

gas
canister   mat

stove

1

Preparing for Siula Grande

*T*his is a true story about two young men who climbed one of the most difficult and dangerous mountains in the world. It is an incredible story of courage and survival.

The two young men were good friends and they had done a lot of climbing together. This had made them feel confident that they knew everything about climbing. They enjoyed climbing, and they enjoyed having fun.

The two friends had climbed several mountains in the Alps in Europe, but the Alps were no longer exciting for them. There were too many other climbers and too many rescue[5] helicopters. They wanted to find a mountain that was more challenging than the Alps. They wanted the climb to be difficult and they wanted to feel alone and free – alone with the mountain. So they chose a mountain in the Cordillera Huayhuash mountain range, a group of mountains in the Andes in Peru.

The Cordillera Huayhuash mountain range is one of the most beautiful and remote[6] ranges in the world. The highest mountain peak in the range is Yerupaja and is 6,634 metres high. The second highest peak is Siula Grande. Siula Grande is 6,356 metres high. Only a few people had climbed Siula Grande before. In 1936 two German climbers had reached the summit – the top of the mountain – by climbing the North Face or side of the mountain.

But nobody had ever reached the summit by climbing the other side of the mountain, the West Face. The West Face of Siula Grande is very difficult and dangerous. A few people had tried to climb it but they had not succeeded. Climbing a mountain by a new way is very exciting. So the two young men wanted to be the first people in the world to climb the West Face of Siula Grande.

They had dreamed about climbing Siula Grande for many months. They did not know what they would find there, high up on the mountain slopes. They did not know that Siula Grande would change their lives forever.

The two young men wanted a climbing adventure that was fun. But when things go wrong, climbing is not fun any more.

This is their story.

My name is Joe Simpson. One morning in 1985, I was lying in my sleeping bag in a small tent. We were camped at the bottom of the Cordillera Huayhuash mountain range in the Peruvian Andes. Beside me, my friend and climbing partner, Simon Yates, was still sleeping.

At base camp before the climb. (Photo: Simpson)

I lay watching the light growing stronger through the red and green material of our tent. Outside a new day was beginning. I thought about the early morning sun shining high up on the mountain peaks.

Our camp was in a very remote place, far from anywhere. The nearest village was twenty-eight miles away. It had taken us two days to walk from the village over rough and difficult ground. All around our camp were mountains covered in ice. And among them was the mountain we had come to climb – Siula Grande.

I got up and went outside the tent. It had snowed a little during the night and the ground was hard and frosty. There was another small tent next to ours. This tent belonged to Richard.

Simon and I had met Richard in a bar in a hotel in Lima, the capital of Peru. We had started talking and Richard had told us about himself. He had travelled all over the world and had many interesting and funny stories to tell. Richard did not know very much about mountains, but he was interested in seeing the Andes.

Simon and I knew that it would take us a few days to climb Siula Grande. We needed someone to look after our tent and equipment while we were climbing. So we asked Richard if he wanted to come with us to the Cordillera Huayhuash. Richard agreed and said that he would stay in the camp and wait for us.

We had set up our stove for cooking underneath a great rock. I filled the stove with petrol and lit it. Then I heated a pan of water to make coffee, and looked around.

Our camp was beside a wide, dry river bed[7]. Across the river bed, less than a mile and a half in front of me, rose a huge wall of ice and snow. This was the Cerro Sarapo mountain. To my left.there was a huge mass of moraines – the rocks and stones left by a glacier[8]. From the moraines rose two other peaks. One of them was Yerupaja, the highest mountain in the Cordillera

Huayhuash. Siula Grande lay behind Sarapo. But I could not see Siula Grande's peak because it was hidden by Sarapo.

Simon came over to the cooking rock and we drank our coffee together. Simon was tall and strong with blue eyes and blond hair. He was a good friend – the kind of friend that you can depend on. He laughed a lot and was ready to see life as a joke. I was glad that Simon and I were going to climb Siula Grande together. We were not only friends, we were also very good climbing partners.

We knew that Siula Grande would be very difficult to climb. So first, we wanted to make sure that our bodies were fit and strong by climbing some easier mountains. We were planning to climb a mountain called Rosario Norte.

'Shall we go up Rosario Norte tomorrow?' I asked Simon.

'Yes,' he said. 'I don't think it will take very long. We'll be back at camp by early afternoon.'

'I'm worried about the weather,' I said.

The weather had been strange since we arrived. Each morning was fine and clear, but by midday, heavy cloud would move in from the east. Then it would start to rain. We knew that high up on the mountain slopes, the air was much colder than in our camp and the rain would turn into snow. This could be very dangerous because a heavy fall of snow could start an avalanche – a large amount of snow sliding down a mountainside. If we were caught in an avalanche it could knock us off the mountain or block our way down.

'You know, I don't think the weather is as bad as it seems,' said Simon. 'Yesterday it got cloudy and snowed. But it didn't get colder and there didn't seem to be high winds on the summits.'

'So do you think we should continue climbing if it starts to snow?' I asked. 'Perhaps the snowfall could turn into a serious storm.'

11

'Yes,' said Simon. 'But we can't stay down here all the time.'

'All right,' I said. 'I'm just worried about avalanches.'

The next morning Simon and I set off on our climb up Rosario Norte. I was feeling very good. I was climbing well and I was feeling healthy and strong. Simon and I both climbed at the same speed, and that was good too. If you have a climbing partner, your speed and level of fitness should be the same.

We climbed higher and higher, until I could not see the camp any more. It was very silent, high up on the mountain. I had a strong feeling of being alone, away from other people. It was wonderful to feel so free.

Simon was ahead of me. 'Look,' he said. 'There's Siula Grande, just north of Sarapo.'

I looked and felt amazed by the huge size of the mountain in front of me.

'It's fantastic,' I said. 'It's much bigger than it looks in the photographs we've seen.'

The summit of Siula Grande had a very unusual shape. It was like a giant mushroom made of snow. Below the summit was the West Face. The west side of the mountain was huge and incredibly steep[9]. It would be very difficult to climb – too difficult for many climbers. But that was why Simon and I had chosen it. We wanted to climb up Siula Grande by a way that had never been climbed before.

There was a long narrow edge running up to the summit of Siula Grande. This was the North Ridge. The top part hung over the West Face. But it was broken into cornices – masses of snow and ice hanging over the ridge – and it did not look very stable[10] or firm.

Huge clouds were beginning to move up over the North Ridge. They were coming in from the east. Already the first snowflakes were beginning to fall. We did not want to get caught in the snowfall, so we went back down to the camp.

Richard was there, preparing the evening meal. We sat up late, chatting and playing cards.

On his way to the Cordillera Huayhuash, Richard had met two Peruvian girls called Gloria and Norma. He could speak a little Spanish so he chatted to the girls. The girls told him that sometimes they brought their father's cattle up to the high pastures[11]. When the girls stayed overnight at the pastures, they slept in some empty stone huts[12] near a lake.

The next day, Richard and I went to see the girls at the huts and bought some milk and cheese from them. The girls told us that they had a brother, Spinoza. We arranged for Spinoza to bring us food from the nearest village.

For the next few days, we stayed in camp, enjoying food and sunshine. But I was getting worried about climbing Siula Grande. What would happen if something went wrong? Perhaps we would die, up there on the slopes. Simon was not worried but he understood my fear. He knew that fear is a natural thing to feel when you are alone on a mountain.

'We can do it, we can do it,' I kept saying to myself.

'OK,' said Simon, finally. 'Let's go tomorrow.'

'How long will you be?' asked Richard.

'Four days,' said Simon. 'Two days for the climb up, and two down. Five days at the most. Try not to worry about us.'

We packed our rucksacks and got ready for an early start the next day. We did not take a tent, because we didn't want to carry much weight on our backs. Instead of camping, we planned to dig holes in the snow to sleep in. But even without the tent, our rucksacks were very heavy. We needed a great deal of equipment – ice screws, crampons and axes, stoves, gas, food and sleeping bags.

The sun was shining early the next morning as we walked towards the West Face. At the foot of the mountain range was a large glacier which we had to cross before we could start our climb. Before the glacier, there was a huge area of moraines.

Richard came with us to the glacier. But it was not easy for him to walk across the moraines because he was not wearing proper climbing boots, only light walking shoes. When we reached the glacier, Richard could not climb up onto it so we left him on the moraines. As we climbed higher and looked down, Richard's figure got smaller and smaller. He looked sad and lonely, sitting there among the boulders[13].

'Take care!' he called.

'Don't worry!' Simon shouted back. 'We'll be back soon!'

2

Up the Ice Field

The glacier was full of crevasses – deep holes in the snow – so we had to cross it very carefully. These crevasses were very dangerous because their openings were often hidden by snow. If we stepped onto this snow there would be nothing under it to support our weight, only empty space. We would fall through the snow into the deep black hole underneath.

The crevasses at the bottom of the glacier. (Photo: Simpson)

That first night we dug a large snow-hole at the bottom of the West Face and slept inside it in our sleeping bags. When we woke at five o'clock the next morning, the weather was freezing. I tried to get out of my sleeping bag but my fingers would not move because I had 'the hot aches'. These terrible pains come when your hands have been frozen and then start getting warm again.

It was getting light and the sky was clear. It was going to be a perfect day up on the mountains. The lower wall of the West Face rose high above us. It was like a huge field made of ice and it was very, very steep. But it also looked very exciting. We put our crampons on and took our ice axes and ice screws in our hands.

'I'll go first, shall I?' asked Simon.

Simon and I were tied to each other at the waist by two pieces of rope, each one was fifty metres long. When you are climbing, you are attached to your partner by a rope and you take it in turns[14] to be the leader. The leader pushes his ice axes – first one, then the other – into the wall of ice above him. He hammers[15] the axes in firmly so that they support his weight. Then he digs his crampons hard into the ice and uses the ice axes to help pull himself up. His partner waits below and when the leader reaches the end of his rope, his partner climbs up to join him.

You depend on your partner completely because you are tied to each other by the rope. So if your partner's axes do not hold and he falls off the mountain, you can be pulled off too. If your partner falls to his death, you can die too.

Simon started climbing up the ice field and I waited below. When he reached the end of the rope, I followed him up. He was looking very calm and relaxed.

'It's steep, isn't it?' he said.

'Yes. But the ice is very good.'

Then it was my turn to lead. I moved slowly up the ice field, feeling confident, happy and strong. The climb was going very well and we had travelled a long way since the early morning. Far below us, I could see our footprints beside our snow-hole in the glacier.

We climbed up the ice field for 300 metres, then another 300 metres. The sun was high in the sky and it was very hot. We took off our jackets and carried them in our rucksacks

Joe climbing the ice field. (Photo: Yates)

on our backs. At last we reached the top of the ice field. As I climbed over the top, I saw Simon sitting on a large rock, waiting for me. He had got out the gas stove and was heating water on it to make hot drinks.

It is very important to drink enough fluid[16] high up on the mountain. If you do not drink enough, you become weak and ill because you do not have enough water in your body. So you need to keep stopping regularly to make drinks. But the only way to get water for the drinks is to melt snow in a pan over the stove. This can take a long time, perhaps even an hour. So sometimes we did not make enough drinks because we did not have enough time.

'Lunch,' said Simon, passing me a bar of chocolate.

I sat back, glad to rest in the sun and look around. It was after midday, and warm. We sat on the rock, high above the huge ice field, which fell like a steep wall below. I looked down at the drop[17] beneath. I felt afraid but I was also excited and enjoying the sense of danger. The first stage of the climb – the

17

ice field – was over and it had not been very difficult. We talked about the best way to climb the next part of the mountain.

Above us were wide bands of rock with ice running through them. We had to find a small gully – a kind of channel in the rocks – which would lead to a wider gully. We had seen a wide gully when we were climbing another mountain and had looked across to Siula Grande.

It was just after midday and it would get dark at six o'clock. So we had just six hours to find the smaller gully, then climb up into the wider gully. There we would dig a snow-hole for the night.

It was my turn to lead. There was a wall of ice coming down over the rocks like a frozen waterfall[18]. I started hammering my ice screws into it but the ice was thin and broke into pieces easily. As I moved up the wall of ice and hammered in the screws, large pieces of ice fell down onto Simon below me.

I tried to climb as fast as I could, but I had to be careful and not make any mistakes. Suddenly something hard and dark rushed towards me from above. It was a huge boulder.

'Rocks!' I shouted as the stone hit my rucksack, then went past me. It was falling directly onto Simon and I was sure it was going to hit him. I closed my eyes as more stones came down the mountain and hit me. When I opened my eyes again, I saw that Simon had put his rucksack over his head to protect himself.

'Are you OK?' I shouted. 'I thought you were hit.'

'Only by small rocks. Let's get moving. I don't like it here.'

I climbed up the last few metres of the ice wall and waited for Simon. He was smiling as he climbed up to join me.

'Where did all those rocks come from?' he asked.

'I don't know. But they were very close.'

'Look,' said Simon. 'There's a gully.'

I looked up and saw a small gully in the rock ahead. It was good that we had found it because now we could climb up

Joe climbing up the wall of ice just before the rockfall. (Photo: Yates)

it into the wider gully. But already it was half past four and there was only an hour and a half of light left. By the time we reached the small gully it was beginning to get dark.

'We ought to find a place to stay the night,' I said.

'Yes,' said Simon, 'but we can't dig a snow-hole here.'

Simon was right. It would be very uncomfortable to spend the night in the small gully. We had to climb further up.

'All right,' I said. 'I'll try and get up the gully before dark.'

'Too late … it *is* dark!' Simon replied.

It was very difficult working in the dark. There was no light except for the beam from the torch which I wore on my head. The night was very lonely, cold and silent, high up there on the mountain. The only sound was the noise of my axe hitting the ice. It took a very long time to climb up the gully, but at last I pulled myself over the top and waited for Simon.

'Let's spend the night here,' he said.

By now it was ten o'clock and a strong wind had started blowing. We were both tired and cross after our long hard day.

We knew it would take another hour to dig a snow-hole.

'The snow isn't deep enough to dig,' I said.

'What about up there?' said Simon, pointing up the slope.

Further up I saw a huge ball of snow, fourteen metres wide, clinging to the rock. Simon moved up to it and started pushing at the snow with his axe.

'Joe!' he shouted excitedly. 'Come and look at this!'

I climbed up to the ball of snow. Simon had made a small hole in the snow and I looked inside. To my surprise, the snowball was hollow[19], like a huge cave. It was almost high enough to stand up in. It was the perfect place to spend the night. Soon we had settled comfortably into our sleeping bags. We had brought packets of dried meals with us. We took two packets out and ate the food and drank some fruit juice.

Our first day on Siula Grande had been long and hard. But we had done some good climbing and we felt pleased. We were confident that we would get to the top the next day.

3

Storm at the Summit

The next morning, I stepped outside the cave and stood on the sloping ice of the gully. I could no longer see the huge ice field which we had climbed the day before. To my right there was a wall of ice reaching up to the top of the gully. I started hammering the ice screws into the ice and pulled myself up. Simon followed me and by one o'clock we had climbed a long way. Our way to the slopes leading to the summit of Siula Grande was now clear.

I felt very confident and relaxed. Now I was sure that we would reach the summit of the mountain. Simon grinned at me happily. He was feeling good too. It was very cold and a strong wind was blowing. We found a place where we could rest and lit the stove to make hot drinks. For the first time, we could see the summit. It was shaped like a mushroom and hung over the slopes nearly 200 metres above us.

The North Ridge, our way down the mountain, lay to the west. But we could not see it clearly because it was covered by clouds coming in from the east.

'It looks as if bad weather's on the way,' I said.

The summit slopes were covered with flutings – thin bands of soft snow which ran steeply down from the top. In most places in the world this kind of snow does not usually stay attached to the high mountain slopes because they are too steep. But these flutings are often found on the Andes mountains. We knew that they were very dangerous. But the only way to reach the summit of Siula Grande was to climb up through the flutings.

There were gullies running between the flutings, but sometimes they were closed off at the top. If we climbed up a gully with no way out, we would be caught in a trap because we would not be able to get back down again.

'I can't see a good way up through those flutings,' said Simon.

'No,' I replied. 'I don't think we'll get to the top today.'

'What time is it?'

'Four o'clock. Two hours of daylight left. Let's get moving.'

We started climbing. I was not feeling so good now. I was leading the way, on the open West Face with a drop of over 1,000 metres below me. Simon was underneath me, tied to me by the rope at my waist. If I fell, I would pull Simon down with me.

Joe climbs the last of the flutings. The glacier is 5,500 feet below.
(Photo: Yates)

Simon entered one of the gullies but immediately he sank up to his waist in deep, soft snow. It was very difficult to climb up through the thick snow. He made his way slowly up the fluting, digging a wide path through the snow as he climbed.

It was beginning to get dark and it had also begun to snow. I was very cold because I had to stand still in one place while Simon dug a way up through the snow. As he dug, he threw the snow down on top of me, making me even colder.

It was now eight o'clock. We would have to dig a snow-hole for the night somewhere on the slopes. When at last I climbed up to join Simon, he was very tired.

'We have to stop for the night,' I said. 'I'm very cold.'

'All right,' said Simon. 'But not here. I'll go on up.'

I waited for another two hours. When I climbed up to Simon, I saw he had dug a large hole in the snow. I got in beside him and we both began digging, making the cave larger. By eleven o'clock we were in our sleeping bags. We had eaten a meal, and had had a hot drink.

'How much further is it to the summit?' I asked.

'Only about a hundred metres,' replied Simon. 'But I've got a problem with one of my fingers. I think it's frostbitten[20].'

I looked at Simon's finger. It was all white down to the hand. It did not look good at all. I felt very worried.

The night was long and very cold. The next morning I awoke early and made hot drinks. The gas flame under the stove was not very strong.

'How much gas have we got left?' I asked.

'One canister,' said Simon.

'It's enough. We'll only need to spend one more night on the mountain. We'll be back at the camp by tomorrow afternoon.'

I went outside and climbed up on to the roof of the snow-hole and then on to the slope of the gully. The weather was much better today – fine and clear, with no wind. I looked up and saw that the gully ended about thirty metres above me. So I would have to cross one of the flutings which ran down each side and get into the next gully.

But which fluting should I choose – the one on the right of the gully or the one on the left?

Simon was below me. Perhaps from his position he could see which fluting was better.

'Which way should I go?' I shouted. 'Can you see anything?'

'Don't go into the fluting on the left. It looks very dangerous,' he replied. 'The one on the right looks better.'

I hammered the axe as hard as I could into the fluting. To my surprise, climbing across it was quite easy. I came out onto the other side and looked up. The summit was only about fifty metres above me. We continued climbing up the gully to the top of the fluting. At last the great mushroom-shaped cornice at the summit was only about sixteen metres above us.

Soon we were standing on the ridge of snow which divides the West Face of Siula Grande from the East Face. I put my axe over the ridge onto the East Face and looked down over it. Simon joined me and we laughed happily together. We had done what nobody else in the world had managed to do. We had climbed up the West Face of Siula Grande and reached the summit. The last part of the climb had been difficult and dangerous, but now everything was fine.

We took off our rucksacks and dropped our axes in the snow, feeling very proud of ourselves. Then we sat quietly for a time and looked around.

'Let's leave the rucksacks here and go up to the summit,' said Simon.

We grabbed some chocolate and walked slowly up to the summit. It was difficult to breathe because of the altitude[21]. The air was very thin at that great height. When we reached the summit, I got out my camera and started taking photos.

I always get a strange feeling of disappointment when I reach the summit of a mountain. I feel it is never as exciting as I thought it would be.

Simon on the summit of Siula Grande. (Photo: Simpson)

'What now?' I thought. 'We've succeeded in climbing Siula Grande, but what's next? We'll have to find a new dream.'

Was that my future – climbing mountains that were more and more difficult and dangerous? I felt afraid when I thought about that. But I had had these feelings before and I knew that they would pass. Reaching the summit of a mountain is also a good moment when you feel happy and proud of what you have done.

'I think a storm may be coming,' said Simon, looking worriedly towards the North Ridge. Big clouds were travelling up the East Face and moving over the North Ridge onto the West Face. They were covering the North Ridge quickly. Already the first snowflakes were starting to fall. We went back and put on our rucksacks, then we started down the East Face.

But after about half an hour we were covered in thick cloud and we could not see our way.

There was no wind, only large heavy flakes of snow falling quietly over us. We stood in silence, staring around us. We had moved away from the ridge, and we did not know which side of it we were on. We were completely lost.

'I think we should get back to the ridge,' said Simon. 'We should try and keep as close to it as possible, away from the flutings. The flutings are very dangerous. If we go down them, we may not be able to climb back up again.'

'But we don't know where the ridge is,' I said.

Suddenly, the clouds lightened and I saw the sun. The sunlight was very weak but I could see the ridge, thirty metres above us. Then the clouds closed in again.

'I've just seen the ridge,' I said. 'It's up there.'

Simon started climbing up towards the ridge. I stood still and waited, holding onto the rope that tied us together. It was snowing more heavily now and I was beginning to get worried. Suddenly, the rope moved as fast as lightning through my hands and I was pulled forward against the mountain. At the same time, I heard a terrible noise from above. Then the rope went tight.

I knew at once what had happened. Simon had fallen over the ridge down onto the West Face of the mountain. But the rope, which was tied to me, had stopped him from falling any further. He was hanging down the West Face.

'Simon!' I shouted. 'Are you OK?'

There was no answer. Fifteen minutes passed, then I heard Simon shouting and I felt the rope go loose again. So I knew that he had got his weight off the rope and had managed to get back onto the mountain. I climbed up towards him. He looked very frightened and his legs were shaking.

'I found the ridge,' he said. 'I only saw an edge of it – far away to the left. But as I climbed, the snow and ice around me broke and fell away. Suddenly I was falling too. I'd been walking over a cornice! Everything happened so fast that I had no time to think. I forgot that I was tied to the rope. I was very frightened. I thought that I was going to die.

'At last I stopped falling,' he went on. 'But I was just hanging there in space. I realized that the rope had stopped me but I didn't feel safe. There was a terrible drop beneath me. I could see all the way down the West Face. At last I managed to pull myself back up to the ridge. When I got there, I heard you shouting from down on the East Face.'

The ridge was very dangerous. Part of it had already broken off. Now the rest of it looked as if it was going to break off too.

4

Accident on the Ridge

We had thought that climbing down the North Ridge was going to be easy, but we were wrong. It was very difficult and it took a long time to go a short way. By the time it got dark, we were still 6,000 metres high up on Siula Grande. We had been on the mountain for over fifty hours and we were very tired. It was snowing hard, and it was extremely cold. A strong wind blew large flakes of snow into our faces. It was dark and the only light came from our head-torches.

'We're not going to get down this ridge tonight,' I told Simon. 'We'll have to dig a snow-hole.'

Simon could not move two of his fingers because they were frostbitten. So I started digging the snow-hole by myself. We were both tired and cold, and feeling angry with each other. The day had been very long. It had started well, and we had been very pleased to reach the summit. But then things had started to go wrong. Both of us had been frightened and shocked by Simon's fall over the cornice.

We ate our last food – chocolate and dried fruit. Simon's fingers looked very bad, but I was not so worried about them now. I knew that the most difficult part of the climb was over. We only had enough gas left to make two drinks in the morning, but it was enough. We would be able to get back down to our camp by the next afternoon.

The next morning the sun was shining and I felt better again. For the first time in four days I felt relaxed and confident. I knew that today was going to be a good day.

We made hot drinks and then started off down the mountain. I was leading and I moved slowly and carefully down the slope of the ridge. Simon followed behind me. We were

Simon rests in the snow-hole on the North Ridge.
(Photo: Simpson)

trying to get to the lowest point of the ridge. From there it would be easy to abseil²² down the next part of the mountain. We could lower ourselves down by a rope.

Suddenly I had a shock. The slope I was climbing down ended and a steep cliff of ice appeared in front of me. I moved carefully towards the edge and looked over it. The cliff was about eight metres deep. It looked very steep but I had to get down it.

I found a part of the cliff which was not as steep as the other parts. I knelt on top of the cliff and drove my ice axes hard into the snow. With my back to the cliff, I slowly lowered my legs over it. Then I kicked my crampons into the ice wall below me. When I was sure that the crampons would hold, I lowered my body slowly over the cliff.

But one of my axes did not feel very secure and I was worried that it would not hold. So I pulled it out of the cliff wall, planning to drive it in again more firmly. But as I removed the axe, there was a sharp cracking sound. The other axe came out of the wall, and pulled me down too. Suddenly I was falling down the cliff.

I hit the slope at the bottom hard. At once I felt a terrible blow in my right knee and the breaking of bones. Suddenly I was sliding down the slope of the East Face but I was still held by the rope so I came to a stop. My left leg was caught up in the rope and I kicked it free. Then I swung around until I was hanging down the cliff against the snow.

Everything was very silent. There was a terrible pain in my right leg. I saw that it was twisted into an unnatural and horrible shape. I pressed my face into the snow and tried to stand up. At once a terrible wave of pain flooded through me. I felt very frightened.

'Have I broken my leg?' I thought. If my leg was broken, it would be very serious. I could not get off the mountain with a broken leg.

Then I thought, 'If I've broken my leg, I'll die here.'

I moved my right knee carefully and tried to bend it. Then I reached down and touched my knee with my right hand. The pain felt like fire. Hot tears filled my eyes and I started to cry. We were in a place that was very remote and far from anywhere. There was no hope of any rescue. We were still about 6,000 metres up on the mountain and Simon would not be able to get me down. He would leave me on the mountain to die alone. When I thought about that, I felt sick and cold.

The rope round my waist had been tight but now it went loose. So I knew that Simon was coming down. Then I saw him standing at the top of the cliff, looking down at me.

'What happened? Are you OK?' he asked.

'I fell. I think I've broken my leg.'

At once his expression changed. He stared at me for a long time, then he turned away sharply. There was a look of pity in his eyes. What was he thinking? Was he going to leave me?

'I'll abseil down to you,' he said.

He came down to me and stood close by me. I saw him look quickly at my leg but he did not say anything. Instead, he reached into his pocket and brought out some pills. They were pills for headaches so they were not very strong. But he handed me two of the pills and I swallowed them.

Simon did not say what he would do, and I did not ask. But everything had changed between us in a very short time. We were no longer two friends working together as a team.

Simon's story

As I followed Joe down the North Ridge, the rope at my waist suddenly pulled me forward. I pushed my axes into the snow as hard as I could to stop myself from being pulled any further. When the rope went tight, I knew that Joe had fallen. After about ten minutes, the rope went loose again. I started to move very slowly and carefully down the ridge.

The rope had disappeared over the edge of a drop. I approached the edge slowly, wondering what had happened. When I reached the top, I looked over and saw Joe below. He was leaning against the slope with his face buried in the snow. He told me very calmly that he had broken his leg. Immediately I knew that he was going to die. Nobody could survive high up on the mountain with a broken leg.

I abseiled down to him and looked closely at his leg. It was very bad and I saw that he was in a lot of pain. There was a look of fear in his eyes. I gave him some pills for the pain. They were not very strong but they were all I had.

I didn't know what to say to Joe. There was nothing that I could say. I didn't know how I was going to get him down the mountain with a broken leg. I could tell him I was going to go and get help but it would be a lie. There was no help in this lonely place, far from anywhere.

So I was thinking that I was going to leave him on the mountain. I looked at Joe. I knew he was thinking the same thing.

I knew it, and he knew it. There was no other way.

The ground in front of us rose slightly, and beyond that, the ridge dropped steeply. Simon wanted to see what was beyond it. I dragged[23] myself very slowly and carefully across the snow to the bottom. Simon was waiting for me, sitting on the rise. He watched me, and for the first time he grinned.

'Is it a straight slope down?' I asked.

'Yes,' he said. I moved slowly towards Simon and when at last I reached him, he put his hand on my shoulder.

'How are you?' he asked.

'My leg's a little better, but it's still very painful.'

'Listen,' said Simon. 'I think I can lower you down the mountain.'

'But how?' I asked.

'We have two ropes, each one 50 metres long. We'll tie them together to make one long rope of 100 metres. We'll tie you to the rope and I'll lower you down 100 metres at a time.'

'But how can you hold my weight?' I asked.

'I'll dig a seat in the snow,' he explained. 'I'll sit in the snow seat and lower you down until you get to the end of the rope. When I can't lower you any further, I'll come down and join you. We'll keep lowering you in this way until we reach the bottom of the mountain.'

I grabbed the two ropes and knotted them together, then I tied myself into the free end of one of them. The other end of the rope was tied to Simon.

'OK. You ready?' asked Simon.

He had dug a deep hole in the snow and was seated in it. I lay on my chest immediately beneath Simon and edged down until all my weight was on the rope, letting my feet hang over the snow. Simon nodded at me and grinned. I lifted my feet and began to slide down the mountain.

Simon let the rope out smoothly as I slid down. I lay against the snow holding an axe in each hand. I was ready to push the axes into the snow if I felt myself falling. After a short time, Simon stopped lowering me. I looked up and saw his head and shoulders, far above me.

Our plan was working! Suddenly I felt more hopeful. Perhaps I *could* get down the mountain after all ... perhaps

The stormy face where Simon lowered down Joe on the rope.
(Photo: Simpson)

I was not going to die a cold and lonely death.

Simon kept lowering me down. Now I could see the glacier which we had walked up five days ago. It curved away towards the moraines and crevasses which led to our camp. It was still 1,000 metres below me and there was a long way to go before we could reach it. But I did not feel so hopeless any more.

Simon stopped lowering the rope and came down to join me.

'What time is it?' he asked.

'Just after four o'clock,' I replied. 'There isn't much time before it gets dark, is there?'

It was very open and windy on the slope. Huge storm clouds were building up and the wind kept sweeping snow against us.

Simon was silent, thinking.

'I think we should keep going down,' he said at last. 'My hands have frozen again. We won't reach the glacier in the light, but I don't think we should stay up here. I don't like the look of this weather. I'll lower you down from here. Will you be all right?'

'Yes. Let's go.'

I slid off the ridge and down the West Face. A storm was blowing and an avalanche of snow rushed over me. I slid faster, and shouted to Simon to slow down, but he did not hear me.

5

A Terrible Decision

A storm was blowing and it was very windy. We were both very cold and tired. I had a broken leg and Simon's frostbitten fingers were very painful. We needed to dig a snow-hole and rest for the night until the storm had finished. In the morning, the weather would be better. But we had not brought enough canisters of gas with us and we had no gas or food left. We were becoming weak from lack of fluid, but without gas, we could not make hot drinks. So we decided not to dig a snow-hole, but to carry on down the mountain.

The conditions on the West Face were very different. It was much steeper than the earlier slopes and I was very frightened. Simon was lowering me too quickly and I was in a lot of pain. I kept shouting at him to stop, but he did not take any notice of my cries.

At last the terrible sliding stopped and I hung silently against the slope on the end of the rope. I managed to hop[24] up onto my good leg then I waited for Simon to come down. While I waited, I started to dig a seat for him in the snow. Digging helped to keep me warm, and I did not think so much about the pain in my knee.

I looked up and saw Simon coming down the mountain.

'We're doing well,' he said. 'We should reach the bottom of the mountain by nine o'clock. Come on, let's start again.'

'All right, I'm ready,' I said. 'But slow down a bit this time.'

But Simon either did not hear me, or he did not want to hear me. He lowered me even more quickly than before. After some time, I had a short rest while he changed over the knot. But then the sliding started again, faster and faster. The pain was terrible, but I continued going down. The sky was full of snow which was being blown by the wind. I could not see anything because of the thick white snow.

Simon came down to join me. 'We're almost down to the bottom now,' he said.

I knew that he was trying to make me feel better. So I put my arm on his shoulder and smiled at him.

'I'm all right,' I said. 'The pain isn't so bad now. How are your hands?'

'They're bad, and getting worse,' he replied.

He started lowering me again. The weather was still bad, but the storm was not getting worse. It was dark but the light from Simon's head-torch flashed yellow off the clouds of white snow. I looked up at Simon so that he could use my head-torch to guide him down.

I was moving down fast. Suddenly the slope began to get much steeper. My heart jumped wildly, and I shouted for Simon to slow down. But he could not hear me. The slope was very steep now and I knew that I was approaching another drop.

'Stop, Simon!' I screamed, but the wind carried my voice away into the clouds of snow. A sense of great danger swept over me. I grabbed my ice axe and tried to dig it into the snow, but the snow was too loose to hold the axe. I could not stop myself and suddenly I was falling, falling into space.

I was sliding over the edge of the drop! I cried out and tried to grab at the snow, but a mass of loose snow rushed over the edge with me. Then I hung in space, my body turning round slowly at the end of the rope. At last the rope stopped turning so I could pull myself up into a sitting position. There was a wall of ice two metres away from me. It was solid ice and very steep. I tried to touch it with my axes but I could not reach it.

I shone my torch further up the wall. The edge which I had fallen over was about three metres above me. Then I looked down to the place where the wall dropped away beneath me.

And there I saw something very frightening – the opening of a large dark crevasse about 25 metres directly below me.

I hung silently on the rope, staring in shock at the terrible drop. After about half an hour, I felt myself being lowered again. I screamed at Simon to stop but my voice disappeared into the darkness.

At last the lowering stopped.

The rope was not long enough for me to reach the bottom of the slope and I could not reach the ice wall. So I knew I had to climb back up the rope, and I had to do it quickly before Simon lowered me again. He did not realize that there was not enough rope to get me to the bottom. My hands were completely frozen and the wind was blowing hard against me. I could not get up the rope.

'I can't climb the rope,' I thought. 'I just can't.'

I felt very <u>helpless</u> and angry. There was nothing I could do. I felt myself growing <u>weaker</u> and I was very cold. I knew that the cold would kill me soon. I thought of other climbers who had died on the mountains. Some of them had not wanted to die and they had fought for their lives. But I did not care any more. I was not even frightened of death. Perhaps the cold had taken away my feelings.

So I hung on the rope and waited to die.

Simon's story

Joe smiled when he slid away from me, but I knew that he was trying to hide the pain. He disappeared quickly down the mountain, out of my sight. I knew that I was hurting Joe every time I lowered him. That made me feel bad, but I could not do anything about his pain. We had to get down the mountain quickly. I was very worried about my fingers. They were so frostbitten that it was getting more and more difficult to move them.

Suddenly I heard a faint cry from below. Then the rope went tight and I was almost pulled out of my seat. I threw my weight back and down into the snow.

'Joe's fallen!' I thought. I let the rope slide slowly to a stop and it pulled tightly between my legs. I waited for about half an hour then I lowered the rope a bit more. But it did not come loose again. So I knew Joe still had his weight on the rope.

My seat was made of soft fine snow, like sugar. It was not hard or firm and it could not hold me for a long time. Suddenly the seat started to move and the snow started slipping away from me. I was being pulled down the mountain in short jerky steps.

It was now nearly an hour since Joe had fallen. I had no idea what had happened to him. Why did he not take his weight off the rope? I could not understand it. I waited and waited but nothing happened. Nothing happened – and nothing continued to happen.

I was shaking with cold and I knew I could not hold the rope for much longer. I began to feel afraid. I was being pulled off the mountain, sliding down over the soft sugary snow. There was nothing I could do to stop the snow from collapsing under me. I knew that I was going to die because I was being pulled off the mountain.

Suddenly I remembered something. I had a penknife[25] in the top of my rucksack. If I could get it out, I could cut the rope. I made the decision very quickly. It was not a difficult decision to make, because I had no other choice. I could not keep my position on the mountain. I opened the rucksack and began searching for the knife. My fingers closed round its handle and I pulled it out. Then I reached down to the rope and cut it.

At once the rope flew away from me into the night. I fell backwards into the snow seat as the rope disappeared. I was alive! I could not think about anything else. Had I killed Joe? Perhaps. But I did not want to think about that.

I dug a snow cave in the mountainside and crawled[26] inside. Then I got into my sleeping bag and went to sleep.

The next day was calm and sunny. There were no avalanches and no wind. The mountains gleamed silent and white around me, and I saw the glacier below me. My fear had gone and I felt calm again. I pushed the roof of the snow cave in with my axe and started to climb down the mountain.

6

Into the Crevasse

I hung on the end of the rope. I was so tired that it was difficult to hold my head up. I knew that I was going to die and I just wanted everything to be finished. The wind swung me round in a gentle circle. I looked down at the black hole of the crevasse beneath me. It was very big – more than six metres wide – and it stretched all the way along the base of the ice cliff. It lay there, waiting for me to fall into it.

The rope above me cut into the cliff edge, causing huge pieces of ice to fall on top of me. My arms and legs were numb[27] with cold and I could not feel them any more. I did not feel any pain and I could no longer think clearly. I only knew I was going to die and I was not afraid. Death would be like a kind of sleep, a sleep without dreams.

The light from my head-torch went out. It was so cold that the batteries had stopped working. Now there was only the light from the stars. I was very glad to see the stars. They were like old friends. They seemed far away, further than I had seen them before. They were like bright jewels, floating in the sky …

Suddenly the starlight went out and I was falling, falling down into nothingness. The rope came suddenly alive and hit my face. I fell so fast that I did not have time to feel anything. It was like falling in a dream with no thoughts and no fear. It was the end at last.

―――――

I fell down and down until something hit my back and I was covered in snow. But I did not stop falling, I carried on. I was falling into the crevasse! I screamed, but the scream died above me as I fell. Then I hit something hard, and a mass of snow rushed down on top of me.

For a long time I lay still, not knowing what had happened. Time passed very slowly, like in a dream. I lay still, with my eyes staring into blackness. I could not breathe easily because of a pain in my chest, and there was a loud noise in my head. Then suddenly my head cleared as the cold air flowed in.

I was alive.

My broken leg was lying bent beneath me. The pain was very bad, but I felt happy. The pain kept burning, and I laughed. Pain meant I was alive. I could not feel pain like that if I was dead. I laughed again, a real happy laugh. I could feel tears rolling down my face.

Then suddenly I stopped laughing and I began to feel very scared. What had stopped me from falling further down into the crevasse? I could see nothing in the blackness. I moved an arm carefully above myself and touched a hard wall. Ice! It was the wall of the crevasse. I continued to move my arm but suddenly it dropped into space. I was on a sloping ledge[28], a kind of bridge. I was not slipping, but I did not know which way to move. I lay with my face down in the snow, trying to make a plan.

'Don't move,' I thought. 'DON'T MOVE.' But the pain in my knee ran through me and I had to take the weight off my leg. So I moved, and at once I felt myself slipping. I knew I had to make myself safe by hammering an ice screw into the wall and attaching myself to it.

My ice hammer was tied to my harness[29] by a thin piece of rope. I pulled on the rope and managed to grab the hammer. Then I hammered an ice screw into the wall and clipped[30] a karabiner – a special clip – to the hole at the end of the ice screw. I took the rope at my waist and after a long time, I managed to pass the rope through the screw. At last I relaxed, knowing that the screw would hold me tight.

I looked up. There was a roof of snow above me with a small hole. I had fallen through this hole into the crevasse.

Light from the moon and stars was shining through the hole. It was good to see the moon and stars but I did not want to look down into the terrible black space under me. I did not want to think about the terrible hole down there.

'I've only fallen a short way down this crevasse,' I thought. 'I can get out in the morning if I wait for Simon.'

Simon.

I remembered him with a shock. Where was he? Was he dead?

'But Simon can't be dead,' I thought. 'I didn't see him come over the cliff.'

I had a spare torch battery in my rucksack. I put in the battery and switched the torch on. Then at last I looked down into the black space under me. The bright beam of light cut through the blackness and shone on the walls of ice. But the light went down and down and was lost in the blackness. I did not know how many metres of darkness were beyond the torch beam, but I felt very scared.

I was in a huge cave of ice and snow. I could only see the outside world through the small hole in the roof, full with shining stars. But unless I climbed up the wall of the crevasse, I could not reach the hole.

I turned off the torch and the darkness seemed even more terrible than before. My only chance of escape from this terrible place was Simon. But Simon was probably dead.

I shouted my friend's name as loudly as I could, and the sound jumped back at me from the walls of the crevasse. Then it died away into the hole beneath me.

The sound of my voice would never be heard through the walls of snow and ice. If Simon was on the mountain somewhere, still alive, he would see the huge black opening of the crevasse. He would know that I had fallen into it.

'SIMON!'

I screamed Simon's name until my throat hurt, and I could not shout any more. When I was silent I tried to think clearly. Simon would not leave the mountain unless he was sure that I was dead. But perhaps he was dead already. Did he fall with me? I had to find out. So I pulled the rope – the rope that had tied me to Simon.

I turned my torch on and saw the rope hanging down loosely from the hole in the roof. I pulled it and soft snow fell down on to me. I felt excited. When the rope became tight, perhaps I could climb up it. So I waited for the weight of Simon's body to come onto the rope and make it tight. If Simon was dead, his body would hold the rope. But the rope did not come tight. Instead, it kept moving easily.

Suddenly the end of the rope fell down beside me. I picked it up and looked at it, staring at it in shock. I didn't want to believe what I was seeing. The end of the rope *had been cut*. I turned off the torch and sat quietly in the dark. I was crying like a child.

'I'll never get out of this crevasse,' I thought. 'I'll die here, all alone in this terrible place.'

I fell asleep, still crying. When I woke, I was terribly cold. I wondered how many days it would take for me to die. Perhaps I could survive for three days. I was sheltered in the crevasse and my sleeping bag would keep me warm. I had not thought about death very much, but I knew that I did not want to die like this.

I sat up and turned on the torch, looking at the wall above the ice. I wondered if it would be possible to climb out. Though I knew that it would be impossible, I had to try. I fought for about an hour, but I could not climb the wall. Each time I started, I slipped back down again. The last time I tried, I fell onto my broken leg. The pain was so terrible that I did not try to climb the wall again.

It was getting light. I looked up at the hole in the roof and checked my watch. It was five o'clock in the morning. In an hour's time it would be day, and Simon would come down the cliff as soon as it was light. I shouted Simon's name again but there was no answer.

A long time later I stopped shouting. It was no good. Simon had gone and he would not come back. I had to make a decision. I had to think about what I was going to do. I was sure of only one thing – I did not want to spend another night on that ledge. Nobody was going to come to the crevasse and find me there. Nobody was going to rescue me.

I had only one chance of survival. Either I could wait to die on the ledge or I could abseil down further into the crevasse. The thought of going deeper made me very scared. I did not want to look down. So I took the end of the rope and threw it down into the space over the ridge. Then I looked at the ice screw which I had hammered into the ice wall. It looked strong and I was sure that it would hold my weight.

I waited for a few minutes. Then I slid off the ledge and started abseiling down the slope. I did not know what was at the end of the rope. Perhaps there was only empty space and I would not be able to get back up to the ledge. But I did not care. If there was nothing there, I did not want to come back.

7

The Return

Simon's story

As I climbed down the mountain, I had a very strange feeling. I felt that there was something evil in the mountains around me and it was watching me. It was waiting for me to die. The mountain had already killed Joe, and now it was going to kill me as well.

Everything was very silent. I stared at Siula Grande rising above me and I wondered why climbing had been so important to us. Now it seemed like we had done a stupid thing. There was no change in the mountain. There was no sign that we had climbed up, across and down it. The mountain was empty, and it made me feel empty too.

I continued moving slowly down towards the glacier. Suddenly I came to the edge of an ice cliff and looked over it. Below me was a drop of at least thirty metres. Then I understood what had happened to Joe.

'Joe must have gone over this,' I thought. 'Oh my God!'

I looked down at the glacier beneath the ice cliff. I was searching for a snow-hole in its surface. If Joe had dug a snow-hole, perhaps he was still alive. But there was nothing there. So Joe was dead. He could never have survived the fall over the ice cliff.

I stared at the glacier in shock. It was terrible to think that Joe had died in this way. He and I had worked so hard to bring him down the mountain safely. We had almost succeeded in getting him to the bottom and we had felt very proud. And then, this terrible thing had happened. It was a cruel way for him to die after such a painful fight to survive.

'I'm going to get off this mountain alive,' I thought. 'It isn't going to kill me as well.'

I began to abseil slowly down the cliff. About half way down I looked below me and saw a deep crevasse at the bottom of the cliff. I stared at it in horror. I knew Joe must have fallen into that terrible black hole.

I was filled with terrible feelings of guilt and could not look down at the crevasse again. I stared at the ice in front of me, thinking about what I had done. If I had not cut the rope, I would have died. I had saved myself, but instead, Joe was dead. How was I going to tell people the truth? How was I going to make them understand why I had cut the rope and killed Joe? Nobody would believe that I had done the right thing. They would only ask, 'But why did you cut the rope?'

I could hear their questions in my mind, but I had no answers.

I abseiled lower and looked into the black opening of the crevasse. But there was no sign that Joe was alive. I could not climb down into the crevasse. I was not strong enough and it would be very dangerous. And I did not want to die in that terrible hole. I wanted to live.

'JOE!'

No answer came except the sound of his name echoing in the blackness. Then there was complete silence. I abseiled down to the bottom of the ice cliff. Then I turned and looked back up. I could see the marks of the rope – the rope that I had cut – at the top of the cliff. I turned away and climbed down to the glacier. When I reached it, I took off my rucksack and sat down.

I realized that I was very tired. We had been on the mountain for six days, and for the last day I had had no food or water. I looked up at the huge West Face of Siula Grande and I knew that I could not climb back up it again. I did not even know if I could manage to get back to our camp.

The glacier was covered with deep and dangerous crevasses. I stared at them, feeling confused and scared. I could not remember the way that we had taken on the way up. Some of the crevasse openings were easy to see, but others were covered in snow. If I stepped onto that snow, I would fall through it into the empty black hole underneath.

I climbed down through the crevasses, expecting to fall into one of them at any moment. But I was lucky and I managed to pass through them safely. At last I reached the moraines and sat down among the boulders.

It was still about four and a half miles to our camp and I was very thirsty. I could smell water all around me but I could not reach it. I remembered that there was water halfway down to the camp. It was in a place where melting snow ran over a huge boulder. So I got up and started moving slowly across the moraines.

After a few metres I turned for a last look at Siula Grande. Joe was still up there, buried in the snow and I thought again about what I had done. But I knew that, if I was in the same situation again, I would cut the rope again. There had been no other way.

I continued climbing over the boulders and stones. Sometimes the stones slipped underneath my feet and I fell. I had no strength left to stop myself from falling. After about an hour I came to the boulder with water. The water shone in the sun as it ran over the boulder. I dropped my rucksack and drank.

Then I set off again, heading for the lakes below the moraines. The camp was not far from the lakes and I would reach it in an hour. Richard would be there and he would ask me where Joe was. I did not want to have to tell Richard about Joe. I was afraid of what he would say.

'But why must I say that I cut the rope?' I thought. 'I can say that Joe fell down a crevasse when we were coming down the glacier. It's stupid to tell the truth about how Joe died. It will only cause pain, and people will think very badly of me. How can I tell Joe's parents what I did?'

I knew that I had been right to cut the rope. I knew that there was nothing else which I could have done. But Joe had died because of my action, and so I felt angry and guilty.

'My friends will believe my story and they will understand,'

I thought. 'I don't care what other people think.'

I passed the lakes and climbed the last of the moraines. Suddenly I saw Richard walking slowly towards me. He was carrying a small rucksack and was bent over, looking at the ground. I stood still and waited for him. When he looked up and saw me, his expression was full of happiness and surprise.

'Simon! It's good to see you. I was getting worried.'

I did not say anything for a moment. Richard looked behind me, searching for Joe.

'Where's Joe …?'

'Joe's dead.'

'Dead?'

I nodded. Neither of us knew what to say and we could not look at each other. I dropped my rucksack on the ground and sat down on it.

'You look terrible!' he said. 'Here, eat this.' He handed me a bar of chocolate. 'I'll make some tea,' he went on. 'I was just coming up to look for you. I thought you might be hurt. Did Joe fall? What happened?'

'Yes, he fell,' I said. 'There was nothing I could do.'

Richard prepared the tea and gave me more food. Suddenly I felt very grateful that he was there. He looked up and saw me watching him and we smiled at each other. Then I told Richard exactly what had happened to Joe. Richard sat silently, listening. He did not ask questions or look surprised. I was glad that I was telling him the truth. When I had finished, he looked at me.

'I guessed something terrible had happened,' he said. 'I'm just glad you managed to get down.'

He took my rucksack and we walked quietly down to the tents.

For the rest of the day I sat in the warm sun outside the tent with my equipment scattered around me. We did not talk about Joe any more. Richard prepared a hot meal, and we drank many cups of tea. I lay half asleep, feeling my body growing strong again.

Towards early evening the clouds came in from the east and it started to rain. Richard brought his sleeping bag and put it in the big tent which Joe and I had shared. He cooked another meal on two gas stoves in the entrance. By the time we had finished eating, the rain had turned to snow and a strong wind was shaking the tent.

We lay side by side in our sleeping bags listening to the storm. I saw Joe's things at the back of the tent. I thought of the storm the night before and what had happened up on the mountain. I knew how bad it would be up there. The snow would be coming down the ice cliff in avalanches. It would fill the crevasse at the bottom of the cliff, and bury Joe's body. As I went to sleep, the picture of the mountain was still in my mind.

Simon, safely back at camp, feels terrible guilt about Joe.
(Photo: Richard Hawking)

8

Out of the Darkness

I abseiled down the wall of ice, going deeper into the crevasse. I looked up at the ice screw which held my rope to the wall. It was far above me and getting smaller.

I was very scared. I wanted to stop abseiling but I could not. I knew only two things – Simon had gone and he was not coming back. So if I had stayed on the ledge, I would have died because nobody would come to rescue me. I had thought about killing myself by throwing myself off the ledge. That would be a quick way to end my life. But I was not brave enough to kill myself in that way. So my only chance of survival was to abseil down deeper into the crevasse.

I did not want to look down. After some time, the slope became steeper and I felt my legs swing suddenly into open space. I was going over a drop. I abseiled slowly down over it until I could no longer see the ice screw. I wanted to cry out in fear. For a long time I hung shaking on the rope. As I swung round quickly, my broken leg hit the ice wall and I screamed in pain and fright. Then I made myself look down.

There was a wide floor of snow about five metres across. I cried out, laughing with delight and relief[31]. I had reached the bottom of the crevassse! Then I stopped laughing and looked at the floor carefully. There were dark holes in it. It was not a real floor after all, just a bridge of snow across the crevasse.

Then I saw something else. About fourteen metres away, a cone[32] of snow rose from the snow floor all the way up to the roof of the cave. It was about five metres wide at the bottom and one and a half metres wide at the top. And at the top of the cone there was a small hole in the roof. A beam of gold sunlight shone through the hole, lighting up the far wall of the crevasse.

This was the way out that I had been looking for!

I slid down the rest of the rope. I had only one thought – I was going to reach that sunbeam. I was going to climb up the cone and get out of this terrible place. I could pull myself up the cone and escape through the hole in the roof at the top. Now that I had a plan, I did not feel helpless any more. It felt wonderful to have confidence in myself again. I felt proud that I had made the right decision to leave the ridge.

I looked at the floor carefully. I had to cross it to get to the cone. The snow was soft and did not look very safe. But there was no other way to reach the cone. I lay on my stomach and moved slowly and carefully over the snow. Sometimes I could hear snow fall away beneath me, but at last I reached the cone. It was high and steep but I would be able to climb it while I was still tied to the rope.

I stood up carefully on my left leg, then I dug my ice axes deep into the snow cone, and pulled myself up. I pressed into the snow with my good leg and then pulled my broken leg up. My leg was burning with pain but I did not want to stop. I moved up the cone very slowly, following the sunbeam.

At last I was directly below the small hole in the snow and I felt my helmet touch the roof. I stood on one leg and pushed my head out through the hole and looked around. It was the most wonderful sight I had ever seen. I had come out about seventy metres above the glacier and there was a ring of ice mountains surrounding me. The mountains were beautiful, more beautiful than I remembered. There was not a cloud in the blue sky and the heat from the sun was very strong. I pushed my ice axe into the snow and pulled myself up out of the crevasse.

I lay on the snow feeling a tremendous sense of relief. The terrible fear which I had felt in the crevasse seemed to melt away in the sun. I had not thought I would ever be able to escape from that terrible place. Now I just wanted to lie in the warm sun on the snow and sleep.

Suddenly I sat up. Although my new world was warm and beautiful, it was as full of dangers as the crevasse. How stupid I was to think that I was safe! The camp was about six miles away and I still had a long way to go. I had to cross the glacier, and then the moraines. But I was not strong enough and I had no food or water. I began to feel afraid again. I started to believe that I was not going to be able to escape. There was something evil in this place which would not let me go.

I could see the moraines in the distance and, beyond them, the lakes. They seemed very far away. But I knew I had to try and get to the camp even if I died on the way. I felt very alone. My head was full of strange voices which confused my mind with different thoughts and ideas. But one voice was different from the others. It was sharp and clear and told me exactly what to do. I knew that if I obeyed[33] this voice, I had a chance to reach the camp.

'First, you have to get to the glacier,' said The Voice.

The snow running down to the glacier was quite smooth. As I began the journey down, I looked up at the ice cliff above the crevasse. Hanging over the top was the rope – the rope that had been cut. I knew Simon must have seen it too.

———

The snow was deep and soft. I pushed the axes firmly into it and leaned on them, pulling myself down the slope. My leg was very painful and I had to keep stopping to have a rest. Suddenly I saw a line of footprints in the snow. So Simon had already come this way and I could follow his footprints. Simon knew the way down. So I would be able to cross the glacier safely without falling into the crevasses.

It was difficult to pull myself across the snow. I lay on my left side and crawled by pulling on my axes and pushing with my left leg. From time to time I stopped to eat snow and rest. All the time I could hear The Voice in my mind. It was telling me to keep moving.

Now it was three o'clock. There was only three and a half hours of daylight left. I was crawling very slowly but I knew that if I obeyed The Voice, I would be all right. I looked ahead and saw a rock rising from the snow. The Voice told me that I had to get to this rock in half an hour. When I reached the rock, The Voice told me to find another target[34] to aim for. So I moved slowly forwards from target to target, crawling faster than before.

Sometimes other voices or thoughts came into my head. I wondered what people were doing at home. I thought about my mother and my eyes filled with tears. Then the words of a pop song came into my head. As I crawled along, I listened to the words repeating themselves again and again. I felt very tired, but I knew that I could not stop. The Voice told me that I had to continue following the line of footprints across the glacier.

The wind was starting to blow. I looked up and saw large clouds rolling across the sky. A storm was coming.

'Go on,' said The Voice. 'Keep going … faster. Don't waste time, go on, before the snow covers the footprints.'

I tried to hurry, lying on my side and crawling as fast as I could. There was snow in the air above, fresh, falling snow. I began to feel afraid. The Voice said I would lose my way. It told me to hurry because soon the snow and the wind would hide Simon's footprints.

The light faded quickly. Night was coming and the wind was getting stronger. I followed the footprints until I could not see them any more. I wanted to sleep but The Voice would not let me stop.

'Move!' said The Voice, 'Don't sleep, not here. Keep going. Find a slope and dig a snow-hole … don't sleep.'

The darkness and the storm confused me but I kept moving forward. Suddenly I fell forward and I knew that I could not go on any more. There was a rise of snow above me. As I dug a snow-hole in it with my axes, I cried out with the pain in my broken leg. Then I crawled into the hole and sheltered from the wind. I pulled my sleeping bag from the rucksack and took off my crampons. It was very difficult getting my broken leg into my sleeping bag and it took a long time.

I could not hear the storm outside any more. I knew that I had to sleep, but I could not because I kept remembering the terrible time in the crevasse. I was also afraid that if I slept I might never wake up again. So I kept my eyes open and stared into the dark. But at last I sank into a sleep that was black and dreamless.

9

The Long Crawl

Simon's story

It was late when I awoke the next day. The sun was shining through the tent walls, making me hot in my sleeping bag. I lay staring at the roof, thinking about Joe and trying to picture his face. He was dead, and there was nothing I could do. I felt an empty pain inside.

Richard was outside by the stove under the cooking rock. He looked at me and smiled. It was a beautiful day. I looked at the mountains in front of me but they no longer interested me. I did not want to stay in this empty place any more. I hated it. It was beautiful but it was also cruel, and it had made me do a terrible thing. I wondered if what I had done to Joe was murder.

Richard handed me a cup of tea and a bowl of food. After I had eaten I walked over to the tent and collected my washing things. Then I went to a deep pool in the river. I took off my clothes and got into the freezing water. I cleaned my body first, then my clothes. As I cleaned myself, I slowly began to feel better. Then I went back to the camp and searched round the tent, looking for the box of medicines. Inside, I found some medicine for my frostbitten fingers and some pills to stop them from becoming infected.

Joe's clothes were lying at the back of the tent. I took them outside and placed them in a pile. Then I put all his personal things in a bag for his parents. I found his diary too. He had written something almost every day, even on the plane from London. Joe liked writing. I looked through the diary but I did not read it. I did not want to know what he had said. Then I found his hat. It was made of wool and was black and white. I knew that he had really liked it so I put it in the bag for his parents.

I had decided to burn Joe's clothes. Richard fetched some petrol and we burnt them in the river bed. When it was over we went *back to the cooking rock and sat quietly in the sun. Richard made a hot meal and we drank cups of tea. We did not talk about Joe. We talked about home and our plans for the future. The empty pain was still inside me. I knew it would never go away, but I could manage to live with it better now.*

I had a bad dream that I was still in the terrible crevasse and I awoke screaming. It was light in the snow cave and very cold. Slowly the memory of the dream faded and a strong feeling of relief washed over me. I moved my leg carefully, and immediately I felt a sharp pain in my knee. I broke a hole in the cave roof and bright sunshine flooded into the cave. The storm was over and the snow lying on the glacier was white and smooth. But the storm had covered the footprints which I had followed the day before.

I rolled up my sleeping bag and packed my rucksack with cold, numb fingers. I was very thirsty. I had had no food or water for two days and three nights. I was not worried about food but I needed water badly. I remembered that we had found a place with water on our way up the mountain. But it was a long way further down, and I did not know if I could reach it.

I started crawling over the glacier. I was very frightened of the crevasses and I crawled very carefully to avoid them. My broken leg dragged behind me. It seemed less painful today and I began to wonder if it was really broken. I pulled myself up and stepped forward onto it. The pain was terrible and I felt the bones slip inside. I lay down in the snow again, staring at the sky.

'Get up ... get moving ... don't lie there ... move!'

The Voice broke sharply through my thoughts. I set off again, crawling towards the crevasses. I got lost many times among the mass of deep holes and covered openings. But at last I saw the dark shape of a boulder and realised that I had reached the moraines. I sat with my back against the boulder, feeling warm and relaxed in the sun. But I was not allowed to rest for very long.

'*Come on, wake up!*' said The Voice. '*Don't sleep. You have a long way to go ... don't sleep ... come on!*'

It was strange to see rocks after so many days of seeing only snow. I decided to lessen the weight on my back so I took all my things out of my rucksack. I left the stove, pan, my helmet and crampons beside the boulder and put only my sleeping bag, camera and torch back in my rucksack.

The moraines near the glacier were made up of very large boulders. I could not crawl round them so I would have to cross them by making small hops on my good leg. I unrolled my yellow sleeping mat and put it on the snow beside me. Then I cut out a piece of the thick yellow mat with my axe and made a splint[35] to support my broken leg. I fastened the splint round my leg with straps from my crampons and my rucksack.

I stood up and leaned against the boulder. I pulled my rucksack on my back and picked up my ice axe. Then I started hopping. At the first hop I fell on my face but I got up and tried again. It took me a long time to go a little way but slowly I started to move forward across the moraines. I tried to use my axe to support myself but sometimes it slipped and I fell down many times. When I fell on my broken leg, the pain was very bad. But after two hours, I turned and looked back at the glacier. Now it was only a white line, far in the distance.

'*Keep going!*' said The Voice. '*Look how far you've come. Just keep going, don't think about it ...*'

I did as The Voice told me. The moraines were an empty place with no colour or life, no insects or birds. It was very silent. I kept hearing songs in my head and I thought all the time about water. I looked ahead and saw an ice cliff. It was only a short distance away. This was the place where we had left Richard on the way up. I sat on my bottom and pushed myself slowly and carefully down the cliff, holding on to the rocks.

I was feeling very good. The cliffs were the last things on the mountain which could have killed me, and now I had passed them safely. But I had to get water. I decided to try and find it. But when it became dark I could not find my way. I had no idea where the water was. The Voice told me to stop and sleep but I had stopped listening to it. At last, at about ten o'clock, I fell and I could not get up again.

'Stop!' said The Voice. '*Stop and rest … you're tired … don't go on.*'

I got into my sleeping bag and fell asleep at once.

Simon's story
The next morning, the deep tiredness which I had felt the day before had gone.

'*Are you feeling better?*' Richard asked.

'*Yes. Yes, much better. It's only my fingers which are still painful,*' I said.

'*I think we should leave,*' Richard said.

When he said this, I felt shocked. I did not feel ready to leave the camp yet.

'*What …?*' *I replied.* '*Yes, I suppose you're right. It's just … I'm not ready.*'

'*Look,*' *Richard said softly.* '*Joe isn't coming back. You know it. We have a lot to do. We have to go to the British Embassy in Lima and tell them about Joe's death. We have to call Joe's parents, and we have to book our flights home. So I think we should go. We need donkeys to carry our things down to the village. I'm going down to see Spinoza and I'll ask him to bring some donkeys up later today.*'

I knew that Richard was right. There was no reason to stay at the camp any longer. So why did I feel that leaving was the wrong thing to do?

Richard started walking towards the river bed.

'Hey, Richard!' I shouted. He turned to face me. 'You're right. We have to leave. But ask Spinoza to bring the donkeys tomorrow morning, not today. We'll leave first thing tomorrow morning. OK?'

Richard turned and walked away. Two hours later, he came back.

'Spinoza will bring the donkeys at six in the morning,' he said. 'Good.'

The walk to the village would take two days and from there we would travel to Lima. We would tell the British Embassy in Lima about Joe and they would help us. I would call Joe's parents and tell them that Joe had died in a crevasse. Later, when I got back to Britain, I would tell them the whole story about how he died.

'Hey,' said Richard. 'We'll need some money in Lima. Didn't you hide your money before you climbed up Siula Grande?'

'Yes. I forgot.' I got up and hurried over to where Richard was standing. 'I put it in a small plastic wallet and hid it under a rock.'

We searched the rocks near the camp but I could not remember exactly where I had hidden the money. At last I lifted up a rock and found the bag of money underneath. There was 195 dollars inside.

'What about Joe's money?' I asked suddenly. 'He hid his money as well. He showed me exactly where he had hidden it.'

'How much did he have?' asked Richard.

'Quite a lot,' I said. 'More than me.'

'You had better find it then,' said Richard. 'We don't know how long we'll have to stay in Lima.'

We looked under the rocks round the camp, but we could not find Joe's money. All the rocks looked the same.

As darkness fell, we felt drops of heavy rain on our tent. We cooked the evening meal on the gas stoves at the entrance. The rain turned to heavy snow and we closed the door of the tent. I was glad that tomorrow the donkeys would arrive and we would leave this place forever.

Later, as I fell asleep, I thought of the snow falling on the glacier beneath Siula Grande. Then the empty pain inside me returned.

10

Journey's End

When I woke the next morning, I had a terrible thought. What if the camp was no longer there? What if Simon and Richard had already gone? Simon must have been back at the camp for two days … there was no reason for them to stay.

I knew that I had to reach camp that day. I checked my watch. Eight o'clock. I had ten hours of daylight ahead of me. I planned to reach the water by twelve o'clock. I pulled my rucksack onto my back and started to hop. I kept hopping and falling, hopping and falling. At last I reached the water. It flowed down from a tall boulder. I pressed my lips to the icy cold water and drank, and at last the terrible dry burning in my throat felt better. I drank and drank.

Immediately I felt a change taking place in my body. I felt fresh and strong again. I knew that the lakes were about three hours' crawl away. I stood up and hopped to the rock for one last drink, then I left. A few metres further on, I saw Simon and Richard's footprints in the mud. I was happy because I felt that I was not alone any more.

The moraines ahead of me were getting smaller but sometimes I still fell. Whenever I felt like stopping, The Voice made me continue. By four o'clock I had reached the first lake. The water looked beautiful with sunlight on its surface. Green shadows shone in its depths and a light breeze blew over it. I lay beside the lake and slept for an hour.

The lake stretched towards the camp like a long narrow ribbon. Then the moraines formed a kind of dam – a barrier across the water. There was a smaller lake beyond the dam. From there, it was downhill all the way to the camp. If I could reach the dam of moraines, I could stand on the top and look down on the tents.

'But will they still be there?' I thought. 'If Simon and Richard have gone, what will I do?'

'*Don't be a fool,*' said The Voice. '*Hurry on … there are only two hours of daylight left.*'

An hour later I reached the second smaller lake and started walking around it. I was sure I could reach the dam before dark. But just as I reached it, I felt huge drops of rain. A strong wind had started to blow and it was getting very cold. A storm was coming.

I climbed slowly up the wall of the dam, using my axe to help me. I was afraid that when I reached the top and looked down, the tents would be gone. When I had reached the highest point of the dam, I leant against a large boulder and looked down. But I could not see anything because the valley below was filled with cloud. If the tents were there, I could not see them. It was almost dark. I put my hands to my mouth and shouted:

'SIIIMMMOONNNN!'

The wind carried my voice away into the white cloud. Had Simon heard me? I did not know. I was terribly cold. I thought about getting my sleeping bag out and spending the night on the moraines.

'*Don't,*' said The Voice.

The Voice was right. If I slept now, I would never wake up again. So I carried on through the darkness, crawling down the hillside. I could not see anything and I had no idea where I was going. After a long time I came to a wide area of rocks and small stones. It was the river bed! I knew that the river lay somewhere in the darkness and the tents were on the other side. But was I moving towards the river or going back towards the moraines?

I looked at my watch and saw that it was quarter to one in

the morning. There was a large boulder in front of me and I leaned up against it. I could not go on much further. I was very cold and I knew that I would not survive the night.

'SIIIIMMMmoonnnn … '

My cry disappeared into the darkness. Snowflakes were falling on my face, and the strong wind pulled at my clothing. I felt warm tears running down my face. I needed someone, anyone to be with me in this terrible night. I could not go on any more.

'HELP MEeeeeeee!'

Suddenly I saw a flash of red and green in the darkness in front of me. It kept on glowing, hanging in the night. It looked like a space ship, but it could not be! Then I heard voices, surprised and sleepy, and saw a beam of yellow light shining out. I felt very surprised and shocked. I tried to move but I could not. Pain ran up my broken leg.

'Joe! Is that you? JOE!'

Simon's voice came out of the darkness. I shouted a reply but nothing came out. Then the light shone over me. Strong arms were reaching round my shoulders, pulling me up, and I saw Simon's face.

'Dying … ' I said in a weak voice. 'Couldn't take any more. Too much for me … thought it was over … please help me.'

'It'll be OK. I've got you, I have you. You're safe …'

Simon pulled me towards the tent and I saw Richard staring at me with a shocked expression on his face. Then they dragged me into the tent and laid me down against a pile of warm sleeping bags. I could see a mixture of pity, horror and fear in Simon's eyes. I smiled at him and he smiled back.

The tent was full of warm light. Richard put a mug of hot tea into my hand but it was too hot for me to hold. Simon took it from me and helped me to sit up and drink it. For a moment nobody spoke. Simon kept looking at me in a shocked way. Then we all started talking at once. I told Simon and

Richard about the terrible time in the crevasse and my long crawl back to the camp. Simon told me about his climb down the mountain. I smiled and touched his hand.

Hours passed. I drank more tea and ate a little food. Simon gave me pills for the pain in my leg. Then he cut away the material of my trousers with a penknife and pulled my boot off. My knee burned with pain and I screamed. We looked at my leg in shock and astonishment. The leg was huge and swollen. The skin was yellow and brown with purple lines running down from the knee. Halfway down it there was a huge twisted lump where my knee had been.

'Your leg is very bad,' said Simon. 'We have to get you to a hospital as quickly as possible. The donkeys are coming in the morning. Richard can go down and ask Spinoza to bring a mule[36] and a saddle as well. Then you can ride the mule to the village.'

'But I need rest and food,' I said. 'I can't ride on a mule for two days.'

'You'll have to,' said Simon sharply. 'It will be three days before you can get to a hospital. If we delay, the leg may become infected. We'll go in the morning.'

I felt too weak to argue. Richard gave me more tea, then left to fetch Spinoza. I was falling asleep but suddenly I opened my eyes again. There was something important that I had to say to Simon.

'Simon … thank you.' I said. 'You saved my life, you know. It must have been a terrible decision for you, to cut the rope that night. I understand that, and I understand why you thought I was dead. You did the right thing. Thanks for getting me down.'

He said nothing. When I looked across at him, I saw that he was crying.

'I thought you were dead,' he told me. 'It was terrible, coming down the mountain alone. I was worried about what

I was going to say to your parents. Your mother would never understand, never believe me.'

'It's all right. It doesn't matter. We're here now. It's over.'

I felt hot tears filling my eyes. Then I slept.

Early the next morning, Spinoza came with the donkeys and mule and we left the camp. After two days we reached the village. The journey was very difficult and the pain in my leg was terrible. Somehow I managed to stay on the mule but I was very weak. From the village we hired a truck to take us to the hospital in Lima. Finally, after two long days, my leg was operated[37] on. The nightmare on Siula Grande was over.

End Note

During the next ten years, Simon and I discussed many times what had gone wrong on Siula Grande. Why did the accident happen? For a long time I was sure that we had done nothing wrong. But finally Simon showed me that we had made a bad mistake. We were trying to carry as little weight as possible on the mountain so we did not take enough cans of gas. But we needed gas to melt the snow down into water for hot drinks.

So we did not look after ourselves properly. We became cold, exhausted and dehydrated. After I broke my leg, Simon lowered me on the rope. We should have dug a snow-hole there and rested for the night. The next morning was bright and sunny. If Simon had lowered me down the West Face the next day, we would have seen the ice cliff and been able to avoid it.

But we had no gas, so we continued down the West Face that night in the dark. The weather was very bad and we did not see the ice cliff. And so both of us nearly died.

When we got home and told our story, some people blamed Simon for cutting the rope. But I do not blame him. He did not know what had happened to me – if I was dead or alive. He had held my weight for as long as he could, but he could not hold me any

*Joe lies at Simon's feet while Spinoza and the girls
prepare to take him to the village. (Photo: Hawking)*

longer. He had to try and save himself. I would have done the same thing if I were him.

Cutting the rope was the right decision; we both survived.

I often wonder what would have happened to my life if I had not had the accident on Siula Grande. Perhaps I would have continued climbing more and more difficult mountains. Many of my friends have died while climbing mountains. Perhaps I would have died too.

After I got better from my injuries, I continued climbing. I wrote a book about what happened on Siula Grande and the story has been made into a film. I have written other books about mountaineering too. In some ways the accident was very lucky for me. Because of what happened, I have become a successful writer and public speaker.

Life is full of surprises.

Points for Understanding

1

1 Why were Joe and Simon interested in climbing Siula Grande? Why was it important to them to climb up it by its West Face?
2 Who was Richard and why did Joe and Simon ask him to come with them to the Andes?
3 Why was Joe worried about the climb? Were Simon's feelings the same, or different?

2

1 What was so dangerous about the glacier?
2 Explain how a climber is dependent on his partner. Why does he need to trust his partner's ability to climb?
3 Why is it important to drink enough fluid on a climb?
4 What went well on Joe and Simon's first day of the climb? What went badly?

3

1 What are the special features of the Andes mountains?
2 Describe Joe's feelings on reaching the summit of Siula Grande.
3 After Joe and Simon reached the summit, something changed. What serious effect did this change have on their climb?
4 Why did Simon fall off the ridge? What stopped him from falling further?

4

1 What surprised Joe and Simon about the North Ridge?
2 'I knew that today was going to be a good day.' How did the day turn out to become a very bad one for Joe?
3 'We were no longer two friends working as a team.' What did Joe mean by this?
4 What was Simon's plan to get Joe down the mountain? What effect did this plan have on Joe?

5

1 Why did Joe and Simon decide to continue going down the mountain?
2 Why did Joe ask Simon to stop lowering him? Why did Simon not do this?
3 Why was Joe in a hopeless situation after he had gone over the drop?
4 This chapter is called 'A Terrible Decision.'
    (a) Who made the decision?
    (b) What was it?
    (c) Why did he make it?
    (d) Why was it so terrible?

6

1 Describe Joe's feelings in the crevasse.
2 How did Joe know that the rope had been cut? What effect did this discovery have on him?
3 What choices did Joe have in the crevasse? Why did he decide to lower himself down further?
4 'If there was nothing there, I did not want to come back.' What did Joe mean?

7

1 Why was Simon sure that Joe was dead?
2 Why did Simon decide not to climb down into the crevasse?
3 How did Simon feel when he reached the water?
4 Why was Simon nervous about meeting Richard? How did Richard react to Simon's story?

8

1 When he reached the snow floor, Joe saw something unexpected. What was it and why did it give him hope?
2 Describe what Joe saw when he put his head out of the crevasse.
3 What made Joe continue on with his journey back to the camp?
4 Joe saw something to help him on the glacier. What was it?

9

1 How did Simon's feelings towards the mountains change?
2 Why did the storm make Joe's journey back to camp more difficult?
3 What did Joe do with the following things?
  (a) crampons
  (b) sleeping bag
  (c) sleeping mat
  (d) rucksack
4 Describe the moraines. Why were they not easy for Joe to cross?
5 Why did Richard want to leave the camp? How did Simon feel about leaving?

10

1 What was Joe afraid of finding at the camp?
2 Why was reaching the water so important for Joe?
3 How did Joe make Simon feel better about what he had done?
4 What mistake did Joe and Simon make on the climb?
5 How has the accident on Siula Grande changed Joe's life?

Glossary

1 **rumour** (page 4)
   unofficial information that may or may not be true.
2 **courage** (page 5)
   the ability to do something that you know is right or good, even
   though it is dangerous, frightening, or very difficult.
3 **survive** (page 5)
   to stay alive despite an injury, illness, war etc. The fact or state
   of continuing to live or exist, especially in difficult conditions, is
   called *survival*.
4 **cope** (page 5)
   to deal successfully with a difficult situation or job.
5 **rescue** (page 8)
   an act of saving someone or something from danger, failure, or an
   unpleasant situation.
6 **remote** (page 8)
   far away from other cities, towns, or people.
7 **river bed** (page 10)
   the bottom of a river, where the ground is.
8 **glacier** (page 10)
   a very large mass of ice that moves very slowly.
9 **steep** (page 12)
   a steep slope rises quickly and is difficult to climb.
10 **stable** (page 12)
   not likely to fall or move in the wrong way.
11 **pasture** (page 13)
   land covered with grass where sheep, cows etc are kept.
12 **hut** (page 13)
   a small simple shelter.
13 **boulder** (page 14)
   a very large rock or piece of stone.
14 **take it in turns** (page 16)
   if people take turns or take it in turns to do something, each person
   does their share of it. The first person does it, then the second
   person does it. Then the first person does it again etc.
15 **hammers** – *to hammer something* (page 16)
   to hit something with a *hammer*. A *hammer* is a tool used for hitting
   things or forcing nails into wood, consisting of a handle and a
   heavy metal top with one flat side.

16 **fluid** (page 17)
   a liquid.
17 **drop** (page 17)
   a distance down to the ground from a high place.
18 **waterfall** (page 18)
   a place where water flows over the edge of a cliff, rock, or other steep place onto another level below.
19 **hollow** (page 20)
   empty inside.
20 **frostbitten** (page 23)
   affected by frostbite – a medical condition in which cold weather seriously damages your fingers, toes, ears, or nose.
21 **altitude** (page 24)
   the height of a place or thing above sea level.
22 **abseil** (page 29)
   to climb down the front of a large rock or a tall building while holding onto a rope.
23 **dragged** – *to drag something* (page 32)
   to pull something or someone along with difficulty, usually because they are too heavy to carry.
24 **hop** (page 35)
   to move forward by jumping on one foot.
25 **penknife** (page 38)
   a small knife with one or more blades that fold into the handle.
26 **crawled** – *to crawl* (page 38)
   to move along the ground on your hands and knees or with your body close to the ground.
27 **numb** (page 40)
   if a part of your body is *numb*, it has no feeling.
28 **ledge** (page 41)
   a narrow surface that continues out from the side of a cliff, wall, or other surface.
29 **harness** (page 41)
   a set of strong bands of leather, cloth, or rope used for fastening someone in a particular place or position or for fastening something to their body.
30 **clipped** – *to clip something* (page 41)
   to fasten one thing to another using a small object.
31 **relief** (page 51)
   a relaxed happy feeling you get because something bad has not happened or a bad situation has ended.

32 **cone** (page 51)

an object with a circular base that rises to a point.

33 **obeyed** – *to obey* (page 53)

to do what a person or law says you must do.

34 **target** (page 54)

something that you try to achieve.

35 **splint** (page 58)

a piece of metal, plastic, or wood that is put next to a broken bone to hold it in place while it gets better.

36 **mule** (page 65)

an animal that has a horse as its mother and a donkey as its father, and is used for carrying heavy loads.

37 **operated** – *to operate on someone or something* (page 66)

to cut into part of someone's body for medical reasons.

Dictionary extracts adapted from the Macmillan English Dictionary © Bloomsbury Publishing PLC 2002 and © A & C Black Publishers Ltd 2005.

Exercises

Vocabulary: meanings of words from the story

Put the words and phrases in the box next to the correct meanings.

> splint   ledge   rumour   altitude   rescue   survival   boulder   clip
> numb   stable   cone   target   glacier   remote   harness   courage

1		the state of continuing to live, especially in difficult conditions
2		a piece of metal, plastic, or wood that is put next to a broken bone to hold it in place while it gets better
3		an object with a circular base that rises to a point
4		having no feeling in a part of your body, because of cold or shock etc
5		a set of strong bands of leather, cloth, or rope used for fastening someone in a particular place or position or for fastening something to their body
6		the height of a place or thing above SEA LEVEL (= the surface of the ocean)
7		not likely to fall or move in the wrong way (this word has other meanings)
8		to fasten one thing to another using a small object
9		a goal or object that you aim for
10		a narrow surface that continues out from the side of a cliff, wall, or other surface
11		a very large mass of ice that moves very slowly

12		to save someone from a dangerous or unpleasant situation
13		unofficial information that may or may not be true
14		far away from other cities, towns, or people
15		a very large rock or piece of stone
16		bravery: the ability to do something that you know is right or good, even though it is dangerous, frightening, or very difficult

Writing: rewrite sentences

Example: *We were in a place that was far away from anywhere and anyone.*
You write: *We were in a remote place.*

1 This is a story of bravery in the face of danger.

2 Our only chance of getting out alive was to descend into the crevasse.

3 Because of the cold, I could not feel my arms and legs.

4 Nobody was going to save us.

5 The air was thin because we were a great height above sea level.

6 I was on a narrow area of rock on the side of the mountain.

7 The mass of snow and ice was not solid or firm.

8 The <u>solid and slow-moving river of ice</u> was covered with dangerous crevasses.

9 We chose a large boulder <u>to aim for</u> and moved slowly towards it.

10 A hammer was tied to the <u>special leather fastening</u> on my back.

Vocabulary & Grammar: fill in the gaps

Complete the story using words from the box. There are two extra words that you do not need.

the	altitude	such	only	I	of	crawl	It	was
glacier	my	mat	cut	looked	around	last	surface	
and	yellow	knee	sometimes	leaned	on	axe	hop	
got	a	but	straps	minutes	fell	very	support	white
numb	to	tried	touched	rucksack	boulders	put		

My leg was broken and I had ¹ .... crawl on my hands and knees. I ² .... coming down the mountain very slowly. At ³ .... I saw a black boulder. I had ⁴ .... seen white snow for many days. I ⁵ .... the black boulder. It was warm and ⁶ .... rested in the sun for a few ⁷ ....

There was one more obstacle in front ⁸ .... me. I had to cross the great ⁹ .... I looked at the white line of ¹⁰ .... glacier. There were many large boulders on the ¹¹ .... of the ice and I could not ¹² .... over them.

My rucksack was a problem. ¹³ .... was too heavy. I could not carry ¹⁴ .... a heavy weight across the ice and ¹⁵ .... I took everything out of my ¹⁶ .... I kept only my sleeping bag, camera ¹⁷ .... torch. I left the stove, the pan, ¹⁸ .... helmet and crampons, along with my sleeping ¹⁹ ....

I unrolled my yellow sleeping mat and [20] .... it on the snow beside me. I [21] .... out a piece of the thick [22] .... mat with my axe. I needed to [23] .... my broken leg, so I wrapped the yellow mat [24] .... my knee. Then I took the leather [25] .... from my crampons. I fastened the mat around my [26] .... with the leather straps.

I stood up and [27] .... against the boulder. I pulled my rucksack [28] .... my back and picked up my ice [29] .... Then I started hopping. At the first [30] .... I fell on my face but I [31] .... up and tried again. It took me [32] .... long time to go a short distance, [33] .... slowly I started to move forward across the glacier. I [34] .... to use my axe to support myself but [35] .... it slipped and I fell down. When I [36] .... on my broken leg, the pain was [37] .... bad. But after two hours, I turned and back [38] .... at the glacier. It was only a [39] .... line in the distance behind me.

Grammar: syntax

Put the words into the correct order to make sentences

Example:	*since we been The strange weather has arrived*
You write:	*The weather has been strange since we arrived.*

1 the altitude was difficult to breathe because of. It

_____

2 I kicked My left leg free and it was caught up in the rope

_____

3 He brought out his pocket and reached into some pills

_____

4 anywhere lonely There was no place in this, far from help

_____

5 My sugar seat was like of snow, made soft fine

_____

6 like dreams of a sleep would be kind without Death

_____

7 there I felt that something in the mountains around me was evil

_____

8 I knew I fell and that I could not go on forward Suddenly

_____

_____

Published by Macmillan Heinemann ELT
Between Towns Road, Oxford OX4 3PP
A division of Macmillan Publishers Limited
Companies and representatives throughout the world
Heinemann is the registered trademark of Pearson Education, used under licence.

ISBN 978–0–230–03445–7
ISBN 978–0–230–53352–3 (with CD pack)

Cover by Jupiter Images/Stock Images

Printed and bound in Thailand

2011   2010   2009
6   5   4   3   2

with CD pack
2012   2011   2010
7   6   5   4   3